The Song Remains the Same

For D.P. Your support and encouragement from across the seas break on ever grateful shores. May the waves of my friendship and appreciation crash with approximate resonance on golden sands distant in miles, but not affections.

James Wilson

The Song Remains the Same

The Hippocrene Society
Neverland Publishing
2012

All text and images © 2012 James Wilson
Book and cover design: James Wilson

All rights reserved, including the right of reproduction in
whole or in part in any form.

The Hippocrene Society
An imprint of Neverland Pubishing
2012

Printed in the United States of America

ISBN 13:
978-0-9826971-5-3

www.neverlandpublishing.com

CONTENTS

Break Into Heaven..1
Driving Southbound..11
Two-Storied Love Song...17
Dawning..21
Stars Will Shine..25
Straits Of Man...29
Belling You...33
Tightrope Walking...37
Good Tidings...41
Teared..47
How Can You Sleep..51
Love Returns...55

{Silences}	59
Fozicians of Bremen	65
{Silences}	69
Breaking Out	71
Drive Harder	77
Moshe	81
Rode Out	87
Redemption	91
High Tide	93
Ice Cold[3]	97
Afterword	103

The Song Remains the Same

'It is better to fail aiming high than to succeed aiming low. We have set our sights very high, so high in fact that even failure will have in it an echo of glory.'

B.N.

†

Break Into Heaven
***

Continuing upstream with the same persistence and perdition as spawning salmon. An ageless tireless odyssey constantly bequeathed. An irrefusable mission that leaves a bubbling wake of 'No!'. Resignation dressed in daring. Indifference masked by staring. Whimpers hid by blaring. Carefree clouding caring. The renegade we must pursue with extreme prejudice has laid the trail before us. He wants to be found. We see traces all around. In destruction, devotion, and just plain deviancy. What we can't see, and what no one will surrender to us, is any kind of identity.

THE SONG REMAINS THE SAME

That is why we embarked on this journey with a weariness unbecoming our youth and vigour. Futility and inevitability sapped our strength. Strange to relate, as we have progressed, we have awoken. The horror and carnage we have seen have forced us to become more alert. The noises emerging from the dark swells of jungle on either bank seem less and less like an external threat and more and more like an internal uprising. Every rustling leaf and every swinging vine portends the confrontation we no longer fear, but crave. Oh, we are wired. Stretched to snap. Amphetamines and adrenaline see us through the nights. We twitch at lurking shadows, howl at unknown sounds. Never get off the boat. We are making caged beasts of ourselves. We use up ammunition out of pure nervous tension. Sometimes we forget ourselves and ask 'Who's in charge here?' The reply, usually accompanied by a laugh of indignation, is 'I thought you were?' But we know full well that the answer lies ahead of us, in our elusive target. The number of attacks increases, but as the frequency rises, the hostility seems to diminish. The violence becomes ritualistic and stylized. Ceremonies of initiation. Teaching us to hear the hypnotic rhythms of gunfire, the melodies of whistling arrows, to appreciate the beautiful colours of spilt blood and viscera. We get the sense we are being given free passage, that we are being spared. Nevertheless, periodically, our men are picked off. To remind us that we are being toyed with or to confirm to those of us who survive that we are exempt? Nobody knows which. We leave our fallen brothers floating face down in the river, a warning to any who come after us (and surely there will be people coming after us, and after them, and after them, and forever) that they may be sickened at our lack of sentiment, but they will reach the same state themselves and had better start preparing for it. As we become inured to the assaults upon ourselves, we become more aware of the utter devastation we are passing through. Our skin creeps, our stomachs heave and wretch. Yet we shiver in anticipation. We see the goal in every smouldering camp, in every wrecked hull, in burnt-down stores and paddies, in flayed corpses, raped women and piked children. We hand back our tickets. Become immune. Relax. There is no way of return. We have seen the steepest pits of horror. We have seen the end. Passed beyond. Now, surely, all that awaits is resolution? We lie down on the deck, close our eyes, and try to meld all thoughts and bodily persistence to the purrs and oscillations of the boat. There is no one at the wheel. To think that our manipulations and manoeuvrings had any influence on the direction of this craft in the first place is infinitely risible. The watch periods and rosters, shifts and duties could've been done away with so long ago. Then one day the engine dies. The boat drifts first towards one bank, then the other, finally becoming lodged in a muddy wallow. As it jolts to a halt, we awake from our mechanized slumbers. We are hit by a stench of pestilence and putrefaction. Flies buzz around decaying flesh of indeterminate origin. We shoulder arms, clamber out the boat, wade through the rank and fetid mud and scrabble up the bank with the assistance of footholds that appear to have been made from clavicles and ribcages. We push through foliage and along what could be a path. From somewhere a rock is thrown, then another, pitching just in front and rolling to our feet. Peering through the jungle canopy, we can see higher ground, caves or fortifications of some kind. What at first appeared to be dappled patches of light and shade now look like the eyes and faces of ghostly beings. Another rock lands at our feet. One of us cracks and screams, starts running and firing into the trees. The rest of us follow. We are here. He is here. This is it. Time to storm the gates. We lash out with a fury and bloodlust that has been fermenting within us from the start. The screams that erupt from our lungs are not natural. They are formless like our rage which struggles to find any direction and is appropriately boundless. All that we have seen and experienced—how could any of us be specific in our ire? I see one companion run himself repeatedly into the face of a cliff; another spins round on the ground, gnashing his teeth, seemingly trying to bite the backs of his own knees. I find myself smacking the butt of my gun against a tree, convinced that I can make it hurt, convinced that the pain will be felt by our target, wherever he is hidden. This abandon goes on until we tire ourselves and blackout. We awake inside the complex of caves. Candles made of fat stand in upturned skulls and cast a dim and sallow light over the walls. Between the tarns and slicks of luminescence loom those ghostly creatures, menacing in their silence and imperturbable expressions. Their stares exude a fierce loyalty and allegiance that keep us shamed to the floor. They look through us as though we aren't there. They look at everything as though it isn't there. They are impossible to reason with. Not that we try. We don't speak a word either. In this realm, a language of words and articulated noises seems redundant. I am becoming suspicious that my thoughts are being read as easily as if they were broadcast out loud. Looking into the dilated pupils of my companions, I know they have reached similar conclusions. We try to sleep for as long as possible and, when awake, actively try to think of nothing. But the constant scrutiny is torturous and the presence of these beings is hideously invasive. We are suffocating; and, it seems, something is being drained away from our personalities—perhaps our very individuality—without our consent. Yet we are fed and watered. Our bodily strength is being maintained. For what purpose is what I want to know. With no natural light penetrating these caves, it is hard to determine how many days, weeks, or even years, we are suspended in this shade of an existence. Our limbs are always left unfettered and one day, whilst picking out bits of dirt from beneath my fingernails, I have the absurd notion that we may not even be prisoners. The idea refuses to go away and I am sure, even in the faltering light of these depths, that I can read the barest trace of a smile on one of the guards' faces. I try to dismiss it. A trick of weakening eyesight; an effect of the noxious vapours released by the burning candles. I go back to sleep. But from now on, whenever I peer into the murk, I think I see that same scintilla of a smile on all the guards' lips. And the more I think I see it, the more it seems to grow, sickening smiles of knowledge creeping over their features like slopped liquids. I stand up. My companions do likewise. I move towards the row of guards at the far side of the cave. They step aside and let us through. They line the walls of the passageways as we pass and, as we get closer to the surface, we hear behind us the mounting rumble of their laughter, a monotone collective bellow that causes the ground to reverberate. Outside, shielding our delicate eyes from the unfamiliar and blinding daylight, we are bumped and jostled, pushed through the pressing bodies of a dense crowd whose whistles and screams pierce our ears, now so unaccustomed to such noise. As we pass through the throng, we fill with energy, urgency and a renewed sense of purpose. We are brought to rest before a crude wooden dais atop of which is a high-backed chair and, behind the chair, a screen. The crowd falls silent. Squinting upwards, we see a figure emerge from behind the screen and take the chair. I have the overwhelming need to fall to my knees and weep. To honour and obey. But someone is pushing my arms out and then, into my upturned palms, a scimitar is gently lowered. The cold face of the blade unleashes a torrent of stroboscopic images in my mind. All the harrowing things I have seen on this journey. The trail of sorrow, anguish and woe. All of it is replayed in an endless instant of wretched detail. It all led to here. It all leads to him. This is what we came here for. This is what we have dreamt of since before we can remember. Revenge? Retribution? The words are too weak. Justice? Deliverance? No. It is something less definite. Something like dissolution. I transfer the sword that I know he has supplied himself to my right hand. I've wanted this for so long, but as I climb the three makeshift steps up to the platform, I do so unsteadily, knowing that he wants this too. His face is veiled in silk. I swing and he falls, never making a sound. I face the crowd, roaring their approval, and am filled with utter dread at the responsibility I now hold. I survey their faithful, loving, obedient faces and am filled with hatred as I unthinkingly sit down in the recently vacated chair.

†

Driving Southbound
***

This isn't driving as recreation. Nor a destination-based sortie. This is driving as distraction. Suck the world in through the windscreen, tread it out beneath the tyres. The need is not for speed, but movement. Sedentary movement. Gather up the ground, siphon in the scenery. Unquenchable need for the same variety. Pylon pylon pylon. Tree. Pylon pylon. Tree. But I think I've done a bad thing. Answer: *Don't think, drive. Just keep driving, boy, and you need never think again. Asphalt anaesthesia. Four-lane river Lethe. Motorway mandragora to keep the troubles all beneath.* Yeah, forget about thinking; or think about forgetting; or both; or neither. I don't know. Nothing fits. Just itches. I could shell my bones like peas. I've got spiderweb face. I'm all over the place. And where did that voice come from? Is this a time for conversation? Is that you Benny? Is that you Charlie? Don't do this to me. I didn't bargain for this. *Oh but you did, boy, oh you surely did: bargained, bartered, begged, and I took your highest bid.* There it goes again! Fading down my mix-ups, speaking over my beds of thought. A buzzing in my ears like some infernal traffic report. *You're getting warmer. For this is. And nor am I out of it. Play with the trifles of men's souls and expect some interference. A hiss and crackle that builds and builds and promises some deliverence!* The city limits seem to hold no limits for me. Pylon pylon pylon. Tree. Pylon pylon. Tree. The telegraph wires flicker in and out the frame of my window. The dial leans to the right of perpendicular. And I feel less peculiar as my thoughts roll one by one away. Trash tossed through passenger windows to race to nought behind. I watch the crash barrier in the middle of the carriageway rise and dip and dip and rise. But this hypnosis isn't strong enough to dull the all behind my eyes. If only I could stop paying attention, I can't help thinking.'To what! To what!' I scream. *Frivolous demands that will only strike terrors into your fainting heart. Just keep driving, boy, and you'll never think again. That's what you paid your toll for; to forget until life's end. Keep on driving and your central reservation will surely disappear and your hazard lights won't chance a guess until your exit's near.* Horizon's asymptote approaching endlessly. Pylon pylon pylon. Tree. Pylon pylon. Tree. I'm a shattered Sadak clinging above the waters that he craves, but there's a rear-view mirror inside me that I can't quite fold away. Everything in the glass has been hazed up and obscured. And there's the faintest ghost of feeling that I thought I had abjured. What did I want rid of, what did I want to flee? I want full disclosure, I hate this secrecy. *Fond worldling, how your heartblood drives with grief. You forget; but cannot forget your forgetting. I will return the knowledge that salves your last pleasure all with pain; but I cannot relinquish what you sold me; for my name is my name.* Three bars, two bars, one bar... two bars, back to three. It seems the countdown markers are playing silly games with me. I'd like to laugh, but I feel the price to pay is rather dear. Still I laugh—thinking nothing's left to fear. And like a rush of headlights; a torrent intense and insistent, everything comes flooding back and I have no resistence. Beauty; love; betrayal; revenge; guilt;

exile. All so fucking mundane. But after driving in such numbness, it is wonderful anguish to feel it all again. *Not goodbye but au revoir. I'll recognize the driver if I don't recognize the car.* The inundation of the senses seems to hot-wire something in my circuitry. Pylon pylon pylon. Tree. Pylon pylon. Three-armed tree. It looks like the footwell has turned to snakes and legless beasts that writhe and creep. I cannot see the pedals and control I cannot keep. My skin feels like it's crawling with invisible lice and ticks; and the memories churn me up inside and make me feel sick. My hands move from the wheel to chase the creeping itch. And soon I'm veering off into a black and screeching pitch. I jolt awake and I'm still driving. Nothing's changed... but yet... This is hell to remember; a torment to forget.

†

Two-Storied Love Song
✳ ✳ ✳

Her fingernails step absent-mindedly down my back. I've forgotten the question she asked, arching in anticipation of nothing I can predict. I'd like to keep this moment in indefinite suspension, ride it out from birth to pension, and find no need to mention all the doubts that plague my mind. But she tip-taps down the rungs of this twisted spine of mine and counts my silence till she counts no more and I run out of time. Flash and a scratch of blinding light and pain. And I'm gone. Ripped from one world to another. A place of unthinking familiarity, a plateau of comforts and problems. Waking beside the warmth of my wife. All the time that I've been gone from here seems like no time at all. Dreams of sensual post office girls linger with worrisome detail. But such dreams will surely slip away, leaving me to bask in the unnerving glow of contrasts. There's a cold breeze through the window; an ice-current of chill. But I'm incapable of closing it off, fearful that where there are barriers, there are other sides. I see myself transmigrated to the ledge, talons slipping for a grip, a chalkboard tapping sound of unbalanced equations with no answers. A raven ruffled, who found no place to land. So they took away his sing-song voice and replaced it with coarse sand. What if all the words I say are now croaked and steeped in death—will I still be able to talk to my children? Or will I waste my breath? Here they are. Questions and permissions. Innocence and wisdom. I still have one song in me. A lullaby. They say that out of grey skies come such beautiful things. And when I sing my last lullaby this is what it brings. A bridge as broad as a knife-edge and as narrow as the desert plains. Chaos breached or brought nearer? And I'm gone. Burnt from ice. Brow mopped by the spine-tingling girl from the sorting office. Delivered or returned? Careful: this parcel is fragile. Yes. RIP away the strips of tape, dig deep

TWO-STORIED LOVE SONG

into the dull envelope, wring the air from lungs of bubble wrap. Keep going. Pick at polystyrene polyps and pustules, tear at tissue paper, crush cardboard backing and untie entrails of string. There's got to be something in there. And when she shrieks at me, 'Is there anybody home?', I don't know where I am anymore. I don't know where I'm at. This might be existence, but is it life? Who is this girl that torments and seduces me so? And what has happened to my wife? If the cloak of conspiracy is the only gown that fits, can I really belong here? I've seen people destroyed by the dance of a dime. I've seen Santa Claus prey on the prostrate and vulnerable. I've had lawmen and medics deny my entire being. I am unravelling and the whole world with me. Ariadne's thread spooling out faster and faster and further into the labyrinth. Suddenly taut. Then slack. And I'm gone. Chiropractor, necromancer, soothe away my pain. Healing hands and light-filled plans to shape me back again. Baby steps… baby steps to bring me home. So, take my hand, child, unsteady as I am, and lead me up that flight, and I'll try to sing my lullaby with the breath that I have left. For I've heard that out of grey skies come such beautiful things.

†

Dawning
***

I breathe the spirit of movement. It's a universal set. Not just locomotion, though that's a part of it. From meditation to instigation, it's animation and inspiration. Oh this energy! Ready the locks and sluices. Flick the switches on. The valves'll get pushed wide open if we let this current run. Lethargy breeds lethargy; and energy begets energy. It can't be destroyed. It just changes form. Entropy doesn't have to be the oath to which we're sworn. If some reverse their circuits, then that's the way that they will course. But don't let them divert you, hold the reins of your own horse. They give rise to friction, they plane against the grain. Then they claim that that is normal and want you to be the same. And if the times in which we're living, they loom over me and you, then we'll breathe in synchronicity and breathe out movement true. We can resist the resistors, conduct the conductors, repeal lawmakers, and induct the inductors. The energy in process, away with change it races; the energy in objects is always locked in places. Oh this energy! So much energy! I'm running up stairs, swinging round poles at the back of buses; I'm clicking my heels as I vault cracks in the paving slabs. ¿Dónde está la playa? Can you see the sun rising higher? Give me stones, I'll be your scryer. Whetstones, keystones, touchstones. More. I hear those angels singing sure. So, shift a shoulder. Roll away the boulder. Let's play risen, not play dead. Call for a showdown where we put an end to the top-down bruck-down. Build from ground level. Look up in wonderment at such an open firmament. Our degrees of separation balmed by the thought that we see the same moon above us. Our degrees of separation no barrier or prevention to us being parts of the whole. An ever-lengthening Chinese dragon; a perpetual Mexican wave; with age-old Spanish customs to stop us being enslaved. And one day such phrases may be fossils from dark

DAWNING

ages bearing the last traces of vanished states and nations. Red-dotted lines erased from the pages of atlases. Communities organic. Not steroid-pumped with panic. To consume more and more. All these imaginary frontiers that greed has conjured up to grate against one another and cause instability all too real. Dissonant tremors; heart murmurs; as mankind flirts with death. Seduced by adverts that depict competition as a figure of strength and health; and an inference that cooperation is some ailing bedridden fool from bygone times. Know this: adverts lie. Know this: the cardiac muscle cells beat stronger together. And now understanding, here comes my intent. Words and actions: the ends to which they're sent. A beam focused with lenses ignites and incenses. One spark is all it takes. One spark's enough to light the fire in everyone. And the light spills and slicks through the dark of continents of strife, illuminating the choking absurdity of dominions all too rife. Those who hold the whips may never get to see; all too often they stay blind for all eternity. We need to shine our lanterns for ourselves, feel the indignation to free us from these spells. Rip it up to start again. Being mistaken is nothing to be ashamed of. Persisting in being mistaken, on the other hand... So am I done with speaker's corner, clarion calls and soapbox shouts? Well, I can't *make you* realize, no matter how loud or often I sound out. Only you can reach that switch. But I hope you come to see; and maybe tap your toes in this endless energy.

†

Stars Will Shine
***

Somewhere and elsewhere and probably all around, the action continues. Drunken revelry, firework displays, fancy-dress pageantry, the indistinct sounds of bands on distant stages projecting into the night and being blown away by summer breezes. Here, we emerge from bivouacs and tepees to sit cross-legged round the fire. Guitars are passed round and, when settled in laps, we start to play on a signal unmarked by words or gestures. Feet tap and hands clap. We all know the song, though nothing's been rehearsed. It seems as though it was authored on another plane that we

THE SONG REMAINS THE SAME

only glimpse rarely... like tonight. We are not a choir. Our voices remain separate and individual. But we sing every line together. The resonance is different for us all; but, as our singing rises into the night sky, mirroring the fire's trail of smoke, we intuit that our many different feelings come from common stock; the basement storehouse of emotion on whose ceiling boards we all walk about unwittingly every day. I now realize I have sung this song many times in the past, and in many different circles (no two of which the same), but after each rendition, the memory fades away, just as it will tonight. These past performances are only ever recalled when the song is played again. And no one is able to (and nor would anyone want to) predict when that might be. These memories pour in from overflowing guttering and runnels into a cistern that froths and foams like the slapping hissing waves in certain caverns and deadmen's holes on seaside cliffs and promontories. The surface furies of this coursing mask the tranquil depths beneath where everything will settle and nothing can be stirred. For the brief duration of our song we are helpless against the surge. The first instinct is to fight. Voices crack and eyes close. But secession is inevitable and soon each of us, in their own way, fills up and floats under. Down into the depths as we sing up to the stars. The limpid atmosphere does not dilute or stretch, but, conversely, achieves a balmy consistency incommensurate with friction. And then, before we know it, we emerge from our song, put our instruments to one side and sit in silence for a while as the fire's embers glow surely down to black.

†

Straits Of Man
***

*I*f I had an island, would it be my land? And then if you came, would it be yours? The trade winds have blown in questions that shouldn't have been posed. And the changes from 'guest' and 'host' to 'owner' and 'tenants' (or much worse) have stuck so hard and fast that they might be impossible to reverse. Perhaps you can understand why I might be slightly abrupt with people that I see waving flags. Banners and pennants, irregardless of the insignia they bear, have all too often been markers of hurt and loss for me. Only the naïve, greedy or vengeful will see the pulling down of one flag and the hoisting up of another in its stead as a symbol for hope. No, usually it just means that the boats come and go from different places. And that the poor people are beaten and executed by men in different coloured uniforms to the last time and with new sets of specially imported machinery. Machinery designed by the most brilliant of minds to bring a seemingly unreasonable efficiency and detachment to the routine slaughter of their fellow men. It's harrowing really. To see paradise ghettoized before your very eyes. I remember when the adjective *tropical* was one that I could adore, conjuring up images of coconuts drifting in azure seas, slowly swept by currents from shore to shore. Life moving at its own unhurried pace. The green swell of life, nurtured by the violent caresses of sunshine and rains. But we've moved from golden dawns on golden sands to a plastic age for plastic lands in one clipped breath of time. And now you are more likely to find, bobbing up and down in the waves, a fridge door or a SIM card. Our technological advancements have given birth to a new era of miracles: you can walk on water now, you can walk straight across the sea—it's a polymer soup, a floating mortuary of design folly. Over-compensating for our species' all-too-fragile physicality, we have become obsessed with permanence and durability. The undegradable container, a symbol for a longed-for potency. And now, somewhere in the Pacific ocean, a new Atlantis is being formed from out of all this clutter that we can't get rid of: the soles of sweatshop sports shoes; six-pack rings; 'disposable' lighters; hooks for shower curtains; a doll's torso; endless varieties of carrier bags. This continent continues to grow and perhaps enough fish and fowl will die in its hideous mesh that their choked carcasses will coalesce into a putrefying strata that, one day, crushed beneath the weight of our own unending detritus, will begin to yield oil. And then, just as sheets of ice and plates of moonrock have been carved up by the dotted-line brigades, so too will this new mess be claimed in the names of squalid sovereigns and myopic ministers.

†

Belling You
***

'Where do you go to at night?' Where do I go to *at all*? For I am not the one on the dunes, cloak billowing and roaring, hair touched with hoar frost and hated by kings. No. I am not the last of the bards, run ragged by the hounds, baying out my final verse to the impatient ravens above. Oh no. I am not the fingers of a man's hand coming forth to play freely with the dripping wax. I am not some false Muhammad, set up in place, beneath an infidel heartland to radiate invisible fire. I am not the brave youth who will ride his horse into the abyss. Nor the one who commanded the sun to stand still. I am not afeard of the rending skies and falling towers. I am none of these things. I am just a witness. And I dissolve no doubts. But I think I might be permitted to set ablaze the cunning and pernicious visions stowed away behind false walls. For destruction is a form of creation. And every creative endeavour I have absorbed now circles, spins and blusters in a cyclone that threatens to rip apart the very fabric of my being. Mezzotint details and blue-screen effects throw out the images that keep widening the cracks. I can see him right now. He tilts back his head and lets the universe gape from his neck. And I'm not supposed to tell anybody what nobody knows. Every living thing steps across the divide alone, unable to hear the imperatives of 'Get over!' and 'Give it over!' being barked from either side. There will be those who slip into the silence—the temptation to fill it with nothing but their own voice being too great for them to resist. They will insist. Forever. Shouting each other down. And there will be those who slip into the silence, craving nothing but an end to their own words. Absurd. Their pain will always be articulated. And I am so far from being immune. Awaking with eyes like saucers and heart trembling like a rabbit nervous not from the whimper, but the

BELLING YOU

bang. Awaking with this pulsing through my veins. The pull of this feeling is all I have known and to give it up seems, at times, illogical. But as I wake up more frequently in places that are not my bed, I am beginning to accept the sacrifice required of me. The man in the moon (weary of the lusts for dusts that saw his brothers slain on earth) may have said it best when he spoke about small steps and giant leaps. We all have to make our own. Preceded by nothing I (or anyone else, for that matter) can assuage. It is the only way we can contribute towards a future that burns not on the spirits of the dead, but on the promise of the living.

†

Tightrope Walking
***

This is a land of confusion, a tangled skein of voices running over and under one another, endlessly intertwining, a writhing mane of gorgon's hair. This is a cross-hatched diaspora and we are lost in the detail, too busy running up and down the paths of our own lines, the beans of an infinite abacus flicked back and forth during a series of difficult (or even unfathomable) calculations. Sometimes we just spin senselessly round and round on the spot, trapped in our own limited fields of orbit, like the banks of featureless players on a table football team, our lack of expressions both symptomatic of and the occasion for a silent gripping terror. But periodically, we slip up, *up and away*: like foil balloons glinting in the sunlight as they race through the atmospheres; or, like jellyfish pulsing up from the deep, their each and every movement bathed in formless grace and celestial glow; or, like lammergeiers rising on thermals unseen; or, like evaporating water molecules breaking free of surface tensions; or, like the purported crafts of extraterrestrial species powered by technologies arcane; or, like superheroes with capes billowing; or, like unfinished similes trailing… And when we float *up and away* like this, we emerge from the detail and gradually see the whole picture unfurl beneath us. And the babble, the chaos, reveals itself to be implausibly harmonious. A harmony of almost unspeakable wonder that runs through every single thing—a white light from which all colours are produced; a mysterious vowel sound that forms the basis of every emotion. We are aware of the rarity of such spontaneous revelation, but constantly yearn from the wellspring of our beings for just such inspiration and enlightenment. We can fall foul of frustrations. But we have also learnt certain rites that can be performed to help send us on our way. On our way, *up and away*. So we load up the donkeys and begin the slow ascent

TIGHTROPE WALKING

into the mountains. Brothers. Brothers and sisters who will stay to finish their game of fantan, seeing not the repetition of divisions, but the repetition of unions. We are, appropriately, a convoy in single file. The track we follow eventually emerges from the gloom of jagged crags and rocky defiles, and breaks into the heady light of the peaks, and a panorama of breathtaking beauty. The searing blues of the sky; the tranquilizing whites of the snow-capped mountaintops and wisps of cirrus cloud; and the mouth-watering lushness of the greenery rolling out in the valleys so far below—this could be enough in itself. But we carry on, collecting as we go the simples we need. On a suitable plateau, we perform the rite, drinking the bitter potable from the same wooden bowl, in the fashion prescribed by tradition. Nausea, vomiting and increased perspiration are not uncommon, the purifying processes often being of strengths that cause such physical knock-ons. The black coals used to heat the alembic are scattered on to the snow in a circular formation where they quickly sink under the duress of their own heightened temperatures. When the snow in the circle has melted, we emerge from the spell and, slowly, but not regretfully, return whence we came.

†

Good Tidings
***

The château stands on the cliff tops of the south side of the island, looming over the lugubrious waves—waves that pound at the black and grisly rocks beneath with the kind of relentless grief or fury one might only have thought possible in the myths of a bygone age. I imagine that the building has always looked deserted—inanimate—an ornate extension to the crags of granite and schist it is founded above and almost seems to founder upon. A silhouette from every angle, it presents a tempting challenge to someone in my line of work and, as I walked back to my hotel from the mayor's office, I pondered why none of the local, regional or even national engineers had taken it on. The financial rewards on offer were not to be discounted as mere shrapnel. Moreover, it seemed to me, such an apparently easy chance to carve a name and reputation for one's self was not something that could be sniffed at. I walked once more to the end of the harbour breakwater and peered out across the straits with my binoculars. The flying buttresses and gothic turrets gave the château the appearance of a cormorant frozen with its wings outstretched. Indeed, I had heard tell of these birds being found in great numbers and corresponding postures all along the surrounding coastline and especially on an outlying uninhabitable archipelago, just north of the island, that the fishermen referred to by the colourful sobriquet of The Skeleton's Yawn. But, strange to relate, whilst there is no marked difference between the terrain of their favoured haunts and that of the cliffs below the château, the cormorants are said to stay well clear of the latter, as though avoiding something polluted beyond redemption. If only the same could be said of the bisquines, luggers and chasse-marées. Not a year goes by, I was told at the coastguard's hut, without some such vessel being smashed to pieces on those same rocks. Everyone knows of the dangers, and lighthouses have long been established on the surrounding outcrops, but still the wreckings continue. The experience of the sea captain, reliability of the craft, even the very weather in the heavens above, are said to count for nothing when these tragedies strike and no discernible patterns have emerged from which blame can be apportioned. The sailors, meanwhile, speak in muted voices of hidden unpredictable currents grabbing boats from miles away and luring them in towards a watery demise made all the more hideous for its inevitability. When I asked questions at the municipality it came as something of a surprise to find that no one knew for sure who legally owned the château—possibly a branch of Roumanian nobility that expired some time in the last century. Nor did anyone have an idea when it was last inhabited. And in the evening I concluded a brief circuit of the quayside taverns with the impression that no one in living memory had even landed on the island, and that it was a place from which the drowned bodies themselves seemed to flee, being washed up miles away on the beaches of the mainland, always, it is said, face down and head first. My sleep was restless, disturbed by the strong local ale, perhaps, or the salacious rumours and tall tales passed round the barrooms for the benefit of my hearing. I dreamt of walking along endless corridors, floorboards creaking, screams of depravity and depredation emanating from behind doors that I daren't push open. I awoke in a feverish sweat and at breakfast the landlord informed me that I had been shouting out in my sleep, just the one phrase, over and over: 'Raise the alarm!' My enthusiasm for the project has now drained away almost completely. Nevertheless, once the routine inspection of the property has been conducted, the paperwork will be signed and my firm will be contracted to install one of our new fully automated beacons in a converted wing of the abandoned château. Success could see our designs for unmanned lighthouses lead the way to a new era of nautical safety. It has, however, taken a great deal of trouble and no small fee to find a ferryman and it looks like it will be a rough crossing.

†

Teared
***

I've got a cat's cradle going, I've built a house of cards. My thumbs are all out twiddled and now they're callous hard. I stare at my shadow till I blink and he makes his escape. I'm surprised he stuck around this long, the past few weeks ain't been great. These lucubrations are wasting me away. When my head hangs heavy and my eyelids start to droop, the double-exposed jurors shuffle in and take their chairs. They sit by the wall and face me in my bed. The three stern characters that have become a familiar sight for whatever time this is in the small hours of the night. They are all pleated by wrinkles;

they match the cracks and scratches in the plaster of the walls. They never speak. They just stare. They seem expectant. Am I to deliberate for them? Well, I've tossed a thousand coins and watched them spin out on the floor. Heads and tails both resolve to leave things as before. So I yawn. What am I accused of? A tired question that has no simple answer. Just a story whose chronology is steadily fading away into a series of images and feelings that are collapsing into one another, threatening to become a seamless jellied mess that will one day evaporate and leave behind it, perhaps, a single muddied pool in which no sense can be divined. Scurf and residue awaits. For now, and not necessarily for better, images and feelings remain. A flick book without finish, an endless stream of pages. And one picture coming to dominate all the others. Whether the picture is repeated many times or occurs just once and lingers, I do not know. Be it frequency or duration, the pain is the same. And the impassive jurors stare on, projecting this carousel of slides and sentiments from somewhere deep behind my eyes. Some scenes lit up by the chill blue X-ray of night; others by the dull rusting warmth of indoors; some scenes scored by shame; others by bitterness and longing. And the image that seeps through them all: a portrait

TEARED

of a girl too good for this world. Laid up in bed, life fast draining out of her, all spent on kindnesses too often unreturned. Naïvely descending into dives and lairs lacking even the company of a songbird to sing shrill of noxious dangers. Hopes routinely snuffed out before the first creaking stair is trod, how she managed to get down into these places with the flame of her lantern still flaring is beyond me. To say we didn't appreciate the light she shone would be putting it mildly. The sudden migraines and nausea erupted in rages—foul-mouthed rants and table-tipping tantrums. Glasses drained and smashed demonstratively. I was the worst of them. A consumptive coughing my disease into others' faces, hoping to finish them off. The only thing that kept me going was a desire for revenge. To teach the woman who left me, all those years ago, what it feels like when the heart freezes to its very core. That desire had long since been pickled in inactivity. But the acrid fumes continued to sweat out my body and the stench saturated all I did. Anyone and everyone bore my revenge now. I roared in that girl's face, relished the tracks of her tears. Felt righteous about stamping out the arrogance of her goodness. She didn't belong here. It was ridiculous. Going from table to table in a starched pinafore to collect nothing but stains. We had made our choices. Still, that boy left with her, though. What was his name? The anaemic-looking one. And he never came back and perhaps that gave some cause for encouragement. Encouragement that I did my best to extinguish over the ensuing weeks and months and years. Unstitching each and every garment that she took away to mend; screwing up each and every epistle that she had dared to leave behind or send. Sure that there are some things that can't be fixed; certain that there are some messages that can't be read. And one night she didn't return. In her stead, that skinny kid. And with unvaunted strength he drags me off my stool and up the stairs. Kicks and pushes me along the street and into a wardroom... to watch her smile at me as she dies. That image. That image. That searing image. And the screening ends. The jurors rise and leave for another night. Do my tears convince them or must I cry again every tomorrow until my sorrow's drained? Again my last companion is a bottle on the floor, it has rolled just out of reach and rests pointing to the door.

†

How Can You Sleep
***

He drums his hands impatiently on the arms of his chair; a constant quest to entertain and be entertained has led to these childlike tics and tantrums. The high captains and chief estates have barely finished wiping their fat fingers on their clothes, picking meat remnants from between their teeth, and belching their corpulent stomachs' satisfaction, when the damsel starts her dance. The girl pleases him and he taps out of time as she twists and turns in front of him, white ribbons trailing from the blonde tresses of her hair. 'Again! Again!' he cries, clapping his hands together. In such moments of glee his features resemble those of a village simpleton and we are briefly reminded that dynastic self-pollination may maintain a family's power structures and jawlines, but that it can somewhat diminish other faculties. The musicians, almost invisible in the shadows, and wondering if they'll ever see their retainers, recommence their playing. Rather beautiful it is too. Later they will state that they have no desire to be the desecrators of graves, and they will refuse to ever play that song live again. But now, they play. And now, she dances. The grace and the horror. The grands battements and brisés felt most keenly somewhere in the bowels of the palace where even the lightest of steps up above ends up rebounding and reverberating with all the dull alacrity of a death rattle. The combinations are clicking into place and dark desires are being unlocked. A feather floating free from flight. A dust mote caught in slanting light. Beauty soon undone by a single parroted request. Every chance of her being remembered... like a vulture pecking livers; a sandman clutching eyes; a jackdaw pulling heartstrings; or blood-heavied marsh flies. 'Bring it on a charger', she says. 'A silver charger', she adds. And she shapes her lips into a moue of consternation that she has learnt to imitate from her mother. Her worry is all about the words being in the right order. They have no meaning for her. Not when the assembled dignitaries gasp and murmur incredulously under their breaths; not when the tetrarch's features fall into ashen hurt; and not even when she is shown, *just minutes later*, the head she requested, revealed to her from beneath a cloche like some rare and appetizing delicacy. No, she'll never be able to understand the connection between the words she repeated and the events that followed. The streams of people who filed out of the towns and cities to walk their grief away beneath the overarching sky of the desert vasts, cheeks bejewelled with tears and the stars above glinting in numbers that have always threatened (and will no doubt continue to do so) to dwarf even the very best of our significations.

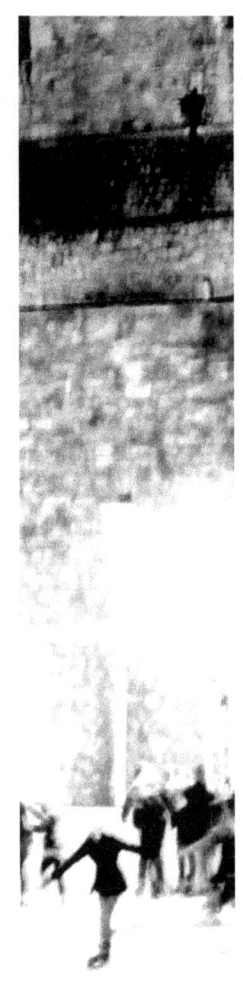

†

Love Returns
***

We're back. What did you expect? Angels with dirty faces? Well, we rubbed ours in the gutters and felt perfectly at home. We bathed in mud and saw the spikenards blanch. Those streets were ours. And now we're welcome. Folded under wings. 'Why is the comeback greeted with more enthusiasm and affection than the ever-present?' do I hear you ask? An interesting question. A question of proof. *Someone* has to disappear to exist. The essence of the return is a simultaneous yearning for free will and the divine plan. Just change 'plan' to 'love', huh? It's natural. Deviate to consummate. Or somesuch malarkey. We did not spend years practising our dismounts for nothing. Swift seamless movements were our speciality. You saw dust clouds in the distance and then there we were *in your faces*, leading our steeds by the halter, and proffering the free hand to your good good selves. (We hope.) If you don't shake it, you're foolish. If you don't shake, we forgive. When we rode out you called us rustlers—now you dub us sheriffs and pin stars to our breasts. One thing you should know: our horses never shied at water. They sure won't shy from this. Absence makes the heart. So, don't call it a disappearing trick—the denigration of a necessity is the kind of base behaviour that ill fits anyone who *knows* us. Yes, stocks rise. Yes, speculation is rife. That's why some stay away forever. They cannot be remembered. Their eternal flights help neither themselves nor others. And those who stay where they are—would we begrudge them that begrudge? Of course not. They might not open their arms quite so readily, but they will surely realize that the feast, the sacrifice, is for them too. And then they will sit down with us. We never wanted people to run on the spot or tread water. Static is anathema. Spinning rocks hurtling through space, shifting seas from side to side. Life moves on for all. The

LOVE RETURNS

longer we were away the more you thought about the possibility of our return. That's some pressure mounting. Some cross to bear. Different does not mean disappointment. Per se. It seemed impossible to come back without being heralded in some way. And that has conjured up an aura of braggadocio; an air of bombast—most of it projected. But boy do we back up words with deeds. We are substantial and when we touch you, you will feel it. This is us. We're back. Swaggering into town with an articulacy and wisdom to shame the so-called educated, the self-styled elite, the scared-stiff establishment. This is us. We're back. The dominican, the devil, the chicken and the cameraman. And the cart we pull behind us is loaded with belief. This is us. And we're back.

{SILENCES}

THE SONG REMAINS THE SAME

{SILENCES}

THE SONG REMAINS THE SAME

{SILENCES}

THE SONG REMAINS THE SAME

†

Fozicians of Bremen
***

We've still got the old groove and, to tell the truth, we weren't expecting to get slaughtered for it! Ok, so it comes between coughing fits and wheezing starts these days, but it's still there and we value it—even if no one else does. We decide to rip up and tear into the newspapers and just enjoy ourselves. We are, after all, a damn fine band of town musicians. We see no point in lingering by the roadside with faces as long as three rainy days, unleashing our self-pity in crows that cut through bone and marrow. No, if you feel the injustices of the world as keenly as we do, you

THE SONG REMAINS THE SAME

don't just hang around to die. You take it on the road and maybe if enough people hear it, things'll change. We might be out of tune with everyone we meet—and our songs of heartfelt protest might just sound like the bitter braying of football fans decrying the ineptitudes of officialdom—but maybe we only have to stay in tune with each other and that will suffice, four vagabonds making a racket that only they seem to enjoy. The key thing being that word 'enjoy'. Making each other laugh and deriving common purpose. Because before, on our own, we were pretty miserable and directionless, accepting fates foisted on us by arbiters that don't have that right. Those referees were wankers blowing for a full time that hadn't yet come. The Satanic mill manager, the huntsman, the mistress and the society hostess—they can all kiss our behinds! Eat our dust. We are heading for towns where we will find better things than death. And even if we never get there, we'll savour every step we take away from those tyrants of the past. We've already had some adventures. Caused some scares. We had settled down to sleep, one night, beneath the broad sweeping branches of a great old yew tree. The dried needles on the floor were a better bed than the bogs and meres, but the cold still dug in with its icy fangs. When one of us spied a distant spark in the darkness, we decided it was worthwhile to investigate. A den of robbers. Or perhaps that should be 'thieves'? I've always found the word 'robber' to be the more romantic choice, wondering if there is hidden away somewhere deep in its etymology a vague value of plundering for a greater good or common cause that simply is not present in the word 'thief'. Robbers or thieves, in the end they passed sentence on themselves. We saw they had a warm hearth and a table laden with plenty enough to share. So we got into formation and began to sing for our supper. It was a fine freeform medley of earthy folk and jazz; spit-and-sawdust stuff that we thought this gang would like. We belted it out and the windowpanes were shivered with so much excitement that they shattered. The men fled from their den complaining of vengeful spirits and unearthly sounds. We took that as a compliment and went to eat our fill and doze off by the warmth of the fireside. The gang returned like thieves in the night, keen to take repossession of 'their' goods. They had no sense of irony and their proprietorial air and brandishing of lucifer matches was, we thought, provocative. There was a bit of a barney. Some blows were struck and they never came back. And you can tell anyone who wants to know that we are still here, warm and contented, town musicians who've still got the old groove.

{SILENCES}

THE SONG REMAINS THE SAME

†

Breaking Out
***

Grow our beards, grow our hair. Shave our beards, cut our hair. Marking time and losing time only end up the same when you get so far. On a chequered floor at the back of a bar, in a former mining town somewhere in the valleys, we just play on, invisible to the crowd. Errand boys between jobs. We didn't expect people to come in from the dark and tell us about jet fighter pilots sent to prospect for oil who got so confused they could only recoil from horrors they'd been told were democratic duties (a conjuror's trick to rival Houdini's). They exhibited symptoms of a syndrome that was hitherto nameless. Now, does a chemical imbalance make everyone blameless? Heaven help us all. I can hear the goats on the hills and they've been made to get restless, the bells on their necks all shaking relentless. Someone ought to tell them to stop their bleating. They don't do enough. Someone ought to tell them to stop their bleating. Now, did that bear repeating? So, here's the fable. A paraclete pricked his ears a little too keenly; he'd been scrying those crystals a little too clearly. He started seeing angels everywhere. Potentially right. He only had one love and that played with his sight. Redux. Reduce to dust. Make new bricks. If the canvas doesn't look right, then maybe turn it over. Or rip it up. Incorporate shreds into new works free of the associations that made it all so difficult before. We're whores. That's always been us. Selling the only thing we value. Again and again. Because we need to get rid of it. And you're buying. Compounds and complexes. Wilderness hideouts. Stir crazy or just plain lazy. After the prejudicial termination of the veil-faced renegade, we just hung around wondering how he did it. Asking after his every habit and hunting out the scraps of paper that he had written his sayings on, handing them out to his ghostly adherents like indulgences, and

BREAKING OUT

with strict instructions that they be secreted away, unread, into the crevices of walls, underneath stones, and in the caverns behind waterfalls. They were frustrating and incomplete glimpses of a methodology that we could never grasp, but would duly come to imitate. Phrases about slugs and razor blades, incinerated pigs and trained cadres. I ordered them to be burned. But they lingered. And later— much too late—I dictated what I could remember of them to a scribe. When they were read back to me they seemed devoid of all their original power, they smacked of faulty testament, and I cried. I found out that he used to ladle water over his shaved head in a ritual that no one could properly fathom. Some believed it was to disguise tears that came to him at regular and predictable intervals; some thought it an ablution; and others attributed it to a need to alleviate his feverish temperature. None of these seemed likely to me. And I didn't need a reason to copy his practice. I used the same ladle and barrel that he had used and knew from the first time that I tipped the water over my head that it was a necessary procedure. Stir crazy or just plain lazy. We eventually got back on the boat. Suddenly longing for the anonymity afforded by a former mining town in the valleys. Suddenly longing for the shelter of an empty bar where we could play a handful of worked songs over and over, waiting for the time when we would be needed once more. Though our mission never ended, disbelief was suspended, and we finally broke back out.

†

Drive Harder
***

Take beautiful inanimate machines from the dreams of technicians unseen, perfect them over the aeons, and have them driven by heroes. That was the plan: pure racing. Corruption is almost natural though. Money and politics do their best to ground even the airiest spirits. He tried to understand anything and everything about him—from the laws of physics to the smile of a child; from when to stay calm to when to go wild—to become a better man. And he came to the conclusion that: he had to drive harder, drive faster, drive harder and drive faster. His racing line was always his learning curve. It could turn circuits into tunnels that were, quite simply, past conscious understanding. It took him on parabolas that scraped the undersides of perfection, chipping away at the smooth translucent surface in such a consistent manner that cracks and fissures were created from which mistakes occasionally escaped. His calculations had always incorporated the possibility of *unexpected things*. But all he could do was drive harder, drive faster, drive harder and drive faster. Asked what it felt like to be a champion, he spoke about peace—the happiness that would come, some distant day, with completion, with wholeness. This genius in the rain brought home sunshine and joys. He shared his victories with the people. And their adoration was sincere. Here was a man who had cut off the circulation of his own arms, for them. And then… No one could touch him, except his father, and gently. (His father was a self-made man.) He poured the celebratory champagne over his own head because even in the excesses of triumph, he was humble and prepared to laugh at himself. He knew the dangerous absurdity of his compelling need. But still he had to drive harder, drive faster, drive harder and drive faster. You've got to drive against the watch, he said. It's about who fulfils the certain distance in the shorter time. Well,

DRIVE HARDER

he pushed his car *beyond* its design capabilities and reached his distance almost too soon. He knew what he was doing. He had been told to expect the greatest gift. There was no knowledge that could make him do anything differently. Surrounded by the eyes of the world and looking so alone, dressed in unfamiliar robes of blue. He had to drive harder, drive faster, drive harder and drive faster. Even the stinking luck of champions runs out. (To be replaced by poetic unjustice.) No New Year's kiss for this or any further year. There would be no fishing trips. He was a fisherman for always. Instant immolation. And as the helicopter rises higher and higher into the skies, the course beneath comes to resemble more and more the image of a body struggling free of its shroud.

†

Moshe
***

I'll always be a stranger in a strange land, perversely, teaching others how to treat aliens. Slow of tongue, I was a rum choice. The kind of man who had always joked, 'I'll write my memoirs when I'm dead!' But, you know, sometimes the unspeakable, the unnameable, *it finds you*. And what can you do? You get on as best you can. I got my sister in. An eye for bling and bluster, she could handle being the mouthpiece and the MC. The front of house business. Leaving me to concentrate on whatever it was I was concentrating on. That ever-consuming fire that was raging me on. The people liked her, my sister, she gave them what they wanted—not, it has to be said, always to their benefit. I'm thinking here of some of the statue commissions she took on at the bidding of immense popular pressure. Sculpture really wasn't her forte. But even so, I don't think many foresaw the fallout of the gold cow piece she made. Melting down the jewellery of members of an oppressed people and recasting it—I think it was supposed to be a commentary on the links between adornment and adoration. Well, whatever it was, it backfired. Massively. The subsequent Inquiry has meant that the ramifications are still with us to this very day in diverse forms of legislation regarding public decency and places of worship. Generally, though, we worked well together, even if our message delivery system seemed, at times, somewhat convoluted. The endless relaying and repeating of the same things. But it was important to get it right. We quickly saw that we had a responsibility. I certainly felt one. It weighed incredibly heavily at times. I could barely lift my hands. I didn't just take on too much. I took on *everything*. It was, as I look back, from my vantage point here on the limbus of the wilderness, leaning on my walking stick, my body caked with age, and draped in a heavy sadness the colour of blue

MOSHE

and purple and scarlet, it was ridiculous. To try and arbitrate all the petty disputes myself. To set myself up as the only problem solver because I felt I had, in some way, been chosen. I was a proud man back then, the stiffest of stiffnecks. And, looking back, I'm still surprised that I had the humility to admit I couldn't cope. To be bawled out and belittled in front of everyone you know by your (first) wife's dad—I'm still amazed that I didn't spark his jaw. And every time I think about it, I get a little shiver of horror at what could have been. How I could have led those people so far astray. Fortunately, it didn't happen that way; and when my father-in-law was screaming up in my face and gesturing all around that 'What you're doing is not good!', I looked about and I saw thousands of expressions and none of them looked especially grateful or happy. They were, rather, confused, impatient and dissatisfied expressions—the expressions of caged animals who were beginning to realize that they needed more than food and drink and shelter. And gazing into these countless different eyes all glazed over with the same inarticulate discontent, I suddenly felt that I could breathe again, that I had surfaced from the close confines of a dark and liquid chamber. And I learnt to delegate. And the expressions of the people seemed to leaven too. They stopped muttering under their breath about 'taskmasters being taskmasters wherever you are' and instead seemed to enjoy their work. They discovered they were cunning craftsmen with a great eye for the beauty of embellishment and the specifics of detail. I look back on that time with great affection. We set in place something to last unto the generations. I have long been aware that I won't see the fruition. My sister's death taught me that: a foretold and functional demise that has left me cold and scared ever since, walking backwards into mine own appointed time. My natural powers, it seems, will last out long enough for another song, then I will turn around and glimpse it. I carved my name in stone, rock carved its name in me. The remnants that remaineth, unmarked they shall be.

†

Rode Out
✱✱✱

I sit on my favourite rock at the end of my beach and contemplate those words you left me with: *'Is this darkness I feel, the darkness you earned*, says the one on the rocks to the one who was spurned'. Your hair got in your eyes as you blew me a kiss. Then away you sailed to the streets I would miss. I've turned those words over thousands of times, but have yet to find a kitemark. Prophetic projection perjured—perhaps. Ironic inversion injured—a lapse? Once a loose tooth, those words are now cankered and so sore that there is almost no chance of finding meaning in or about the rotting and figurative skin flaps that conceal their painful and stunted roots. I'm guilty. I'm not guilty. I have no conviction in my judgments. I've been on this island and I've been on my own, frazzled by suns that have scorched dreams of home. Home: an indistinct and desperate longing that pounds dully and ceaselessly, like the rays upon my closed eyelids. At night, when I can rest from suchlike squinting, I fantasize about artificial light. Lampposts hunched like overzealous butlers, keeping loneliness at bay. Lampposts cowering like mute witnesses. Lampposts threatening to sing. To sing of the shadows that dart between their watches. To sing of the shades that cannot evade their piercing scrutiny. To sing of the crimes of the street. Ah and oh the street! How I yearn for the streets. Glutinous tarmacadam abrading my face, please mix with my blood in my very last scrape. The gentle and regular lapping of the waves spitefully mocks the pulsing of traffic at night. The constellations above illuminate darkness with patterns provided by my own cortical modules. And I'm hankering after neon and the nascent threat of sex and violence. This station is slowly becoming unmanned. It seems that inevitable isn't quick enough. And the final accelerant comes in the form of an unbidden footstep pressed into damp sand—the sign I've awaited to start going mad. I've

RODE OUT

been thinking: How many ways can a man kill a man and can you think of a way without dirtying your hands? The footsteps proliferate overnight. I take a stick of koa wood back to the cabin and fashion a makeshift cudgel. Then I break it in two and burn it on the beach, scared it could be used against me. The trees have taken their sides. They watch and wait for my demise. I cut them down piecemeal and systematically, feeding the branches into bonfires in the evening. It's no use. There are two distinct sets of prints now—one small and one larger—and my hope and my fear is that they are manifestations from some other world. A parallel island where you walk with a parallel me on a parallel beach by the parallel sea. My fear is that that's no crumb of comfort, just a guarantee, of my apparent desertion in this reality. If I'm on the rocks, may I break your hull, in a parallel world where you never feel whole. If you gave me this darkness, I hope you drown in the slick, in that other dimension where you mix with the sick. And any which way and any which how, I know the only thing that I can do now… is miss you; just sit here and miss you; disappear incompletely and miss you.

†

Redemption
***

We retreat to our cells and I wonder when did this home become a hermitage? The silence cascades and courses all about, cold as winter streams, slaking no one's thirst but its own. If the world is to freeze about me, I shall be like the robin who flew through the banqueting hall. Darting from out of one wintry expanse and swiftly flying into another, relishing all the while his few moments of comfort. I will not dwell on the darkness. Unwanted but never undone, my shoes are free of laces. They couldn't bear my strength. And my determination won't succumb to such a superficial force as gravity. Independent or abandoned; I'm still not settled on it. My doosras, googlies and chinamen all spin towards the positive; but that doesn't mean my heart's not stumped. The truest lessons we always learn alone. I thank you for teaching me that. I understand pain now. You're a glacier pushing me away. You will make mountains and valleys. Beautiful landscapes will reveal themselves from beneath the ice sheets. Perhaps I was foolish to think I could help. But if I am just fragmented stone; discarded scree; so be it; I will still look skywards as I tumble down from the peaks; and if I ever come to rest, I will be a founding stone; sure and steady; for those who need me; and maybe one day that will be you.

†

High Tide
✳✳✳

It makes me ache with age and weariness, but I still remember when I set off to get my news from those bootleg vendors down by the lock. I don't know whether to be sad or to rejoice at the distances since covered. Distances that have nothing to do with space or years. Distances that are, it seems, something more akin to the mysterious sprawling cycles or currents of the great oceans deep. High tides and ebb tides that have crashed me violently against the shores only to drag me back with dull and steady insistence to then crash me down once more in places far-flung yet faintly familiar. It was never about the act of selling and buying. Transactions at the lock were never on that level. It was more a question of whether enthusiasm and passion could continue to be accepted as currency. Well, they are still in circulation, but, in days of constant market uncertainty, I'm not sure they keep the same value for long. Maybe we only have room for one big passion in our lives. It might burn itself out as quickly as a struck match. Or, it might linger for ages like a puddle of meltwater. Either way, all else becomes filtered through it into fractals of varying diminishing scales and intensities. And I still don't know whether to be sad or to rejoice; grateful for the heights at which I have soared, or forlorn to have been unable to reach them again. I remember what the vendor said when taking receipt of my payment: You know, you can read good news or bad news into any given event and, for you, they are both the same—this crucifixion was staged. There is no way that a victim cannot know long in advance what is about to happen. It is impossible for them to think that they are just clambering up a wooden pole to admire the view. I heard this news and then I listened. The tales of dancing girls; bouquets of flowers taped here and there like at some accident black spot; and requests for hands to be thrown up in the air—

they could only be confirmed much later, once the vaults of the East were opened. The reports of mass exodus, tears and jeers still, even now, remain in the realm of rumour. The evidence that survives reveals us tourists from the future to be the ones acting out most shocked and full of anger—just as the agents had instructed us to behave so that we would fit in. But I think the agents might have got it wrong. I'm sure I can still hear pockets of the faithful exhibiting love (even as the horror plays out in front of them). I don't know. Perhaps my hearing is affected by a tinnitus of hope; and perhaps my sight is sometimes too keen. Nevertheless, I have seen the scenes and I have seen: a second-string line-up lost and shrinking on a stage that's far too big for them. I have seen the scenes and I have seen: an unfettered chain gang facing and digging in different directions, like a flock of starlings, ready to take flight at the next loud bang. I have seen the scenes and I have seen: an exit from the filthiest business needing a fitting demise—and they delivered. I have seen the scenes and I have seen: the waves at the lowest ebb still continuing to follow the same inimitable movements as those that broke at the highest of high tides. I have seen the scenes. And I will see again.

†

Ice Cold [3]
***

We are emotionally incompatible with endings, is what I have finally [*sic*] come to believe. 'What happens *then?*'; 'What happens *next?*'; 'What happens *after?*' ask the children at the conclusion of the tale told. Well, none of us have really grown up and none of us has managed to crawl very far from that curiosity tree. (Have you ever spoken with those who lack the inquisitive spirit—their words and features seem somewhat submerged beneath a sort of settled sheen of inertia, a eunuchoid gloss. Their thoughts and deeds sluggish with hideous indifference. Ruminants of mindfat.) Those questions should stay with us forever and always beg to be applicable. Undrowned kittens distressed in a sack. Let them out you callous bastards! […] and have you ever noticed how people look up and to the left when they try to grasp a new idea, and up and to the right when they are seeking to express an existing one? Well, sometimes I look up to left and right all day and I've got the bruises to prove it. My approach is clumsy and haphazard, roundabout of course—all preamble and daydream. My chronologies tend to deal with states not dates, so my explanations and narratives can sound muddled—but I know when they feel right. What I'm trying to say is that we walked away to walk our ways; we went indeed to do our deeds. Our futures were not, as you may have suspected, stillborn and flushed out to the beds of deep green seas. We walked away and if you plot our paths on your charts you'll see our different directions perhaps resembling the wilting petals of a flower at summer's end; or the fading glorious colours of a spidery firework. But more than that they come to resemble the lines of longitude, looping round the globe. Meridians marching out then merging back as one, at the poles. Some cycles move on scales and routes that are, quite simply, ineffable. And finishes

ICE COLD 3

frustrate us. The sheer incomprehension of saying that something was but is now not. What if it's more a case of some things *are* then some *forgot*? We shuffled off to walk our ways; but it could all come again one day. They say love's a circle with no end; so don't terminate with hate my friend […]

AFTERWORD

By the time The Stone Roses returned in late 1994 with the comeback single, *Love Spreads*, and second album, *Second Coming*, I was a fully-fledged fan feverish with expectation and I rushed out to buy both single and album on their respective days of release from my local branch of Woolworths in West Norwood, London. A year later I was lucky enough to see the band play live at the Brixton Academy at one of my first ever gigs and one that remains one of the finest I have experienced. My affection for the music of the *Second Coming*-era Stone Roses is no less to that

THE SONG REMAINS THE SAME

I hold for their earlier material. For me, their two studio albums complement each other like night and day or winter and summer. When I felt the need to formulate a creative response to the songs of The Stone Roses, I hadn't intended to break their career or musical canon down into different sections... but I soon realized that their later material was far more tied up with their story as a band and my experiences of living through that story, as a fan, and in the end it felt right to think about two different projects.

AFTERWORD

The writing processes for this collection were the same as for my earlier book, *All the Colours Fade*—and I quote from that work's 'Afterword': 'The pieces were written whilst listening to the music of The Stone Roses—usually different versions of the song in question on repeat play. Sometimes a degree of free association initiated the process; sometimes I started writing bringing a backlog of images before I began. In either case formless fancies were honed, however minimally, into a semblance of narrative.'

As with *All the Colours Fade*, other influences emerged, either tied with the songs of The Stone Roses from the start, or becoming attached at a later date. The writings of Guy de Maupassant, Christopher Marlowe, Emanuel Swedenborg, Joseph Conrad, Franz Kafka, Bram Stoker, Jacob & Wilhelm Grimm; the Book of Exodus; artworks by Fra Filippo Lippi and John Martin; and the films of Richard Kelly, Adrian Lyne, Francis Ford Coppola, Asif Kapadia and Victor Sjöström, all filtered through to some degree.

I would like to thank Donna and Joe Font at Neverland Publishing for their work and continued support; Paul McAuley and his website <<http://

www.thisisthedaybreak.co.uk>> for helping to confirm which direction the piece 'How Can You Sleep' would take and for introducing me to the enlightening Fra Filippo Lippi painting; and a big thank you to Devon Pearse for once again being a willing test case reader. Words do no justice to the gratitude I must express to Ian, John, Reni, Mani, Robbie, Nigel and Aziz, for the songs and shows that have provided such constant inspiration and pleasure.

JW, January, 2012

One love to all the Roses community who have made 2012 such a magical year, especially those at Paul Stevens' excellent Don't Stop website and forum <<http://www.stoneroses.eu>> and those I have met at the Roses' triumphant comeback gigs across Europe.

JW, July, 2012

James Wilson is the author of *All the Colours Fade* (Miami, FL: Neverland Publishing, 2012) and *Images of the Afterlife in Cinema* (London: Duchy of Lambeth, 2011). He is the translator of two volumes of the French writer Guy de Maupassant: *To the Sun* and *The Foreign Soul & The Angelus*. His prose fiction has appeared in the journal *The Use of English*. He lives in London.

www.ingramcontent.com/pod-product-compliance
Lightning Source LLC
Chambersburg PA
CBHW061332040426
42444CB00011B/2890